and its
MYSTERIOUS
MARKET

Getting Started &
Doing Business
in the
New Russian Marketplace

Stanislav Tverdohlebov, Russia
and Thomas P. Mullen, U.S.A.
Editors

The Association of Foreign Economic Cooperation
for Medium and Small Business, The Production-
Creative Union <<D.A.H.C.>>, and
New York University, Leonard N. Stern School of
Business

TRADEWINDS PRESS, U.S.A.

Published by

TRADEWINDS PRESS
1 Closter Commons
Box 400, Suite 140
Closter, New Jersey, 07624, USA

This publication is designed to provide accurate and authoritative information in regard to the subject matter covered. It is sold with the understanding that the publisher is not engaged in rendering legal, accounting, or other professional service. If legal advice or other expert assistance is required, the services of a competent professional should be sought. *From a Declaration of Principles adopted by the committee of the American Bar Association and the Committee of Publishers.*

The publisher offers discounts of this book when ordered in bulk quantities. For more information, contact TRADEWINDS Press.

Printed in the United States of America
10 9 8 7 6 5 4 3 2 1

ISBN   0-9631202-0-4

Dedication

To Mr. K. TAZAKI

Contributors

V. Costenko (Russia)

V. Kulkov (Russia)

V. Markov (Russia)

T. Mullen (U.S.A.)

I. Rostovanov (Russia)

A. Sheljagov (Russia)

J. Stanton (U.S.A.)

Edited by

Stanislav Tverdohlebov and Thomas Mullen

Contents

Introduction

Getting Started

2.1   Relationship-oriented but...

2.2   Capitalism but...

2.3   Reject Bureaucracy but...

2.4   Market-oriented but...

2.5   Tips for Managers Doing Business

Getting Started

3.1   Inofirm businesses

3.2   Foreign investments

3.3 Legal Foundations for Investments Activities Act

3.4 The commercial rate of the ruble, and currency transactions

3.5 Hard currency transaction regulation

3.6 Trade and services rendered for the free convertible currency

Getting Started

4.1 Establishing documents

4.2 Joint venture registration

4.3 The relationship of the joint venture with the soviet organization's founder

4.4 Joint Venture material-technical supplies

4.5 Realization of the joint venture goods and services on the USSR domestic market, and abroad

4.6 Financial issues related to the joint venture's activities

4.7 Taxation and income allocation

Appendix 2
>   Some additional considerations on the type
>   and rate of tax privileges for Russian
>   enterprises with inofirm participation

Appendix 3
>   Directory of Russian Agencies

INTRODUCTION

Perhaps the single greatest challenge that a non-Russian business person faces when deciding to do business in Russia or in any of the other republics within the Soviet Union is understanding a completely new set of fundamental business attitudes and practices. In a recent *U.S. News and World Report* (Sept. 9, 1991) it was noted that the Russian Republic has moved boldly to remove a host of restraints on commerce. This book is intended to introduce business people to these changes in laws, regulations, customs, and cultural dynamics in order to do business more effectively in the new Russian marketplace.

Russia and Its Mysterious Market: Getting Started & Doing Business in the New Russian Marketplace was written by individuals from a variety of fields, including Russian experts in the legal, political, and economic fields and by members of the faculty and staff at New York University. It answers basic questions of initiating and conducting business in Russia which may be useful to Western enterprises interested in establishing a business relationship in the Russian marketplace.

Specific questions addressed in the book include:

1) What fundamental legal changes have

taken place that will lead the country toward a market-oriented economy?

2) What are the fundamental issues in transferring money out of the Soviet Union?

3) What are the questions which need to be addressed when registering a company in Russia?

4) What is the process for establishing a joint venture in the Soviet Union and why is a joint venture desirable from a Russian perspective?

5) What are some of the basic guidelines for importing into and exporting goods out of the Soviet Union?

6) What are some of the key cultural dynamics which need to be recognized when establishing, negotiating, and maintaining a relationship in Russia?

In developing the book we have included specific information on many of the most significant changes in the business environment. Undoubtedly some of these specifics will continue to change. Indeed, given the rate of change, no book could hope to capture all the necessary information about the situation at any point in time. However, in selecting the topics on which to focus, we have tried to choose areas which are either representative of underlying practices and attitudes or areas which are likely to remain relatively constant for some period of time.

It is our hope that the book will serve to de-mystify the Russian marketplace and by being introduced to this information now, managers will be better prepared to understand and assess the business environment as it evolves and be better able to establish productive working relation-ships.

The original idea for this book come from personal discussions with Mr. W. Meinecke, the Chairman of the Observation Council of the German Academy of Management. This book elaborates on discussions and reflections from meetings with business people from Germany, Great Britain, Japan, Italy, Saudi Arabia, and the United States. The contributors and editors are especially grateful to Mr. K. Tazaki for his valuable advice.

Finally, it is important to note that we have chosen to use the words Soviet Union and Russia interchangeably in much of the text. We are not saying that Russia and the Soviet Union are the same. Obviously they are not. We have used the words interchangeably because much of what is true for the Soviet Union is true for Russia. In our discussions.throughout the book we have attempted to address emerging issues in Russia by focusing on those aspects of Soviet economic activity which apply to the Russian marketplace today.

In preparing the book, a particular thank you needs to go to John Willig and his colleagues at TRADEWINDS Press. When we first met with John, we had what can best be called a very rough draft and some ideas. Through the very determined efforts of the folks at TRADEWINDS, we believe the book has been crafted in such a way that it is significantly more accessible to readers worldwide.

S. V. Tverdohlebov, Moscow, 1991
T. P. Mullen, New York, 1991

SECTION 1

LEGAL FOUNDATIONS
FOR DEVELOPING
MARKET-ORIENTED RELATIONSHIPS
IN RUSSIA

The development of market-oriented relationships in the Soviet Union has required the formation of new economic structures and practices which are being created within the context of world economics. It has required the Soviet Union to establish new legal foundations that support the reorganization of its present management structures and systems with new economic methods in order to function within a global economy.

As a necessary prelude to these changes, a new legal code for Soviet foreign economic relations has been worked out and adopted. It both emulates international law and transforms the management of foreign economic relations from an all-embracing centralization to a federation model.

This new economic legislation broadens substantially the Republics' rights to control foreign economic activities. This expansion includes the control of currency and credit policy, quotas and licenses, export specialization, and registration of foreign economic entities. The adopted legislation is divided into two basic categories:

1) those laws of immediate action that regulate the functions reserved to the All-Soviet Union: i.e. customs and currency laws; and,

2) those laws of specific condition that apply to each of the Republics: i.e. foreign investment regulations.

The basic outlines of the currency policy were enunciated in November, 1990 by the Union-Republic Currency Committee which consists of the President of the Cabinet of Ministers of the USSR and the Presidents of the Union-Republics. The regulations regarding the implementation of international settlements, as well as changes in the ruble rate, were determined in December, 1990 by the Council of the State Bank of the USSR which controls the new banking system. The Council consists of the President of its Board and the heads of the state banks of the Union-Republics. Based on the same principles, the Union-Republic Customs Barter Board was formed to define the customs list and the level of customs taxes to be levied on Soviet imports and exports.

These new legislative acts were passed to replace departmental instructions in many fields.

The laws adopted, in accordance with the Constitution, should result in the substitution, abrogation, or reduction of departmental instructions. Finally, these acts clearly outline the legal capacities of the participants in economic activities, submitting them to the law and simultaneously providing them legal protection.

What does the new code of foreign economic legislation specifically address? At its core is the USSR Custom Tariff Law which regulates foreign goods within the context of the internal market and allows budget projections of customs income. This law sets import and export taxes. In the case of both imports and exports, the list of taxed goods (as well as the extent to which they are taxed) depends on the varying economic conditions based on supply and demand within the the various republics. It allows both foreign competition in the internal market and fair protection from competition in specific Russian industries.

The new USSR Banking Law is important, as well. The law establishes control over the ruble rate in relation to foreign currency, declaring it the exclusive prerogative of the State Bank of the USSR, but ends the banking monopoly of the Vneshekonombank in the sphere of international settlements. As of December, 1990 the law conferred banking rights on each Union-Republican bank, on specialized Union banks, and on commercial banks licensed by the State Bank of the USSR. Now that both Soviet and foreign enterprises are allowed to select the banker of their choice, competition is beginning in this field.

The new currency legislation clearly defines the rights and commitments of Soviet and foreign enterprises and citizens to possess and command foreign currency in international settlements within the USSR. At the same time, declaring the ruble the single legal means for payment within the USSR has stopped the "dollarizing" of the Russian economy. The ruble has increasingly been introduced into international exchange through payments for imports.

Finally, the new investment legislation substantially broadens the forms and spheres of application for foreign capital in the USSR. It provides investors with a guarantee of normal economic activities within the Soviet Union while it integrates foreign investments into the process of privatization. It also allows investments to be channeled into loans acquisition, instead of the use of bank credit which can only increase the foreign currency debt of the country.

With the approval of these laws which allow a Russian market-oriented economy to take its place in the global economy, the preparation of the new legal foundation is has been established. The laws provide the equivalent of state insurance to Soviet enterprises that assume commercial risks in their foreign economic activities. The next step in this process is to approve legislation regarding collateralized loans (the Law of the Pawn) as no such mechanisms are readily available in the current business environment. This new legislation should not only untie the hands of Soviet enterprises in the international credit market, but also become the foundation of normal credit activities in the internal markets of the USSR.

While changes continue, the legal foundations and social mechanisms have been put into place to move Russia to a market-oriented economy and a member of the world economic community.

Getting Started

The move from centralization to a federations model has expanded the republics rights to control foreign economic activities.

The accrediting bodies have created new legislative acts that outline the legal capacities of the participants in these economic activities.

USSR Customs Tariff Law

- sets the list of taxed goods
- sets import/export taxes
- allows for foreign competition in the internal market

USSR Banking Law

- ends the USSR State Bank's monopoly in international settlements
- establishes the USSR State Bank's control of the ruble rate
- allows Soviet and foreign enterprises to chose their banker

The new currency legislation

- allows international settlements between Soviet, foreign citizens and enterprises

- declares the ruble as the only legal means for payment

The new investment legislation

- allows greater opportunity for foreign capital in the USSR
- integrates foreign investments into the process of privatization

SECTION 2

THE RUSSIAN PARADOX[1] -
A NON-RUSSIAN PERSPECTIVE:

Understanding the Current Cultural Environment

Many members of the Russian business community today are caught between a set of old, well-established dynamics and a set of new, emergent dynamics. The old practices are characterized by the reality of a highly centralized, heavily politicized, communist state. The new direction is characterized by a vision of a decentralized, market-oriented, non-communist state. Because the former was a reality rooted in three generations of the society and the latter is based on hopes built upon limited experience and exposure, these changes create paradoxes -- contradictory qualities and aspirations -- which simultaneously pull many Soviet business people in opposite directions. *Both the old and the new however are aspects of the Russian culture and value system today.*

E.T. Hall explains that culture functions as a

---

[1] Portions of this chapter are based on an earlier article by E. Beliaev, T. Mullen, and B.J. Punnett titled, "Understanding the Cultural Environment: U.S.-U.S.S.R. Trade Negotiations," *California Management Review*, 27:2, p.100-112.

selective screen between the person and the outside world and designates what we pay attention
to and what we ignore. People evaluate the behavior of others on this basis; consequently, misunderstandings arise when they interact with others
whose frame of reference is different from their
own.[2] R.D. Robinson describes this as "culture
shock" induced by the removal of familiar cues
and by being confronted by "unexpected behavior
and institutions and by different values and world
perceptions."[3]

*In many ways the Russian business
community is experiencing culture shock
with itself as the old clashes with the
new. A key factor to negotiating a business deal and sustaining a business relationship is to understand these paradoxes
and how they are likely to affect the business process.*

2.1 Relationship-oriented but...

There seems to be general acceptance in the
business community that Soviet business people
are relationship oriented. In their application processes for the licensing of foreign firms the
Soviet licensing agency requests information

---

[2] E.T. Hall, *Beyond Language* (Garden City, NY: Anchor Press,
1977).

[3] R. D. Robinson, *International Business Management-A Guide
To Decision Making* (Hinsdale, IL: The Dryden Press, 1978).

about previous dealings in the Soviet Union and intentions about establishing long term ties with the Russian Republic. Similar to the Japanese, Soviets attempt to get to know the potential partner in a variety of settings and from a variety of perspectives. This approach runs counter to other cultures which are seen as significantly more time conscious and task oriented. Americans and others stress the need to "get down to business", that 'time is money", and that the passage of time without concrete results is frequently wasteful.

With all this emphasis on relationships, however, Soviets (especially during negotiations) have been characterized as unsympathetic, uncompromising, combative, and manipulative.[4] As a result, while on the one hand, Russians are relationship-oriented, on the other hand they are frequently seen as argumentative and adversarial in business settings.

This paradox suggests that companies considering doing business with Soviets be prepared for a difficult negotiation process. *Keep in mind that time taken during the negotiation process to establish relationships will pay dividends over the longer term.* Establishing such relationships, however, does not

---

[4] M.N. Rajan and J.L. Graham,"Nobody's Grandfather was a Merchant: Understanding the Soviet Commercial Negotiation Process and Style," *California Management Review*, 33:3, p.40-57.

necessarily translate into undue compromising. Rather it translates into mutual respect and understanding coupled with a genuine interest in the conditions which the Russian partners are facing and the long term goals of the Russian enterprise. As George Hamilton, Senior Managing Partner for International Business Development for Polaroid recently commented, western companies should worry more about developing long term relationships than rushing to repatriate profits.[5]

2.2 Capitalism but...

Former Foreign Minister Eduard Shevardnadze recently commented that Soviet skepticism of a proposed joint venture with Chevron Oil Company was understandable. While personally endorsing the venture, he noted that the fears surfaced by the proposed 25 year, multibillion dollar deal were understandable since, "it has been dinned into our heads since childhood that capitalists do nothing but rob other states by buying up their wealth for peanuts."[6]

On the one hand there is a desire to embrace capitalism. On the other there is a fundamental mistrust of what the implications of this shift are. This, coupled with an ideologically and, at times, culturally driven distrust of outsiders can

---

[5] *New York Times*, September 1, 1991, p.6.
[6] *New York Times*, August 16, 1991, p.1.

combine to undermine activities at any stage of the business relationship. The recently liberated Soviet free press may in some instances aggravate this problem in particular situations as it has with the Chevron deal. Well developed relationships can serve to overcome many of these hurdles, but as noted earlier, these take time and energy to develop.

This paradox suggests foreign business people should be sensitive toward appearing to sell capitalism. *In the next section of this book, managers will note that in applying for a license for doing business in the Soviet republics, there is a section which requires the foreign applicant to address the question of how the suggested business will assist or cooperate in the development of Soviet organizations.* Recognizing this as a fundamental concern and developing an understanding of what a meaningful response is to this concern can foster the type of long term relationship referenced earlier. This concern is highlighted by one seasoned executive's comment that, "Companies that worry only about taking out short term profits can feed the nation's distrust of capitalism that started 100 years ago."[7]

---

[7] *New York Times*, September 1, 1991, p.6.

2.3 Reject Bureaucracy but...

As noted earlier the Russian business person is going through a form of culture shock as familiar patterns and institutions collapse and new patterns and institutions emerge. In the process, many members of the Russian business community are caught between the old and the new and, in the process, the old and more familiar may be more comfortable. What is familiar to three generations which have known only Communism is that all individual and collective action is overwhelmingly influenced by state ideology and the state.

While the state ideology (communism) has been expunged by popular demand, there is significant evidence that the Soviet state is being replaced by the Republican state. In many ways this is to be expected because of the interconnected nature of the economies between the republics, the inbred value system which subverts the needs of the individual to the needs of the society, the long standing political and geographic issues which threaten to flare up, and perhaps most importantly, the lack of a viable alternative to centralized government.

The emergence of a federation of republics and the recognition that no one republic can go it alone is an implicit recognition of this interdependency. So while centralized control under the

Communist Party has been rejected, it is recognized that much of what works in each of the republics is based on a centralized system of controls and an acceptance of mutual interest.

This paradox suggests that organizations seeking to conduct business in Russia be prepared for a smaller, somewhat more local, but still very viable bureaucratic structure. Clarifying this expectation for senior management and for the team assigned to do business in Russia *at the beginning of the process* can help the team to plan accordingly in order to more effectively overcome the inevitable obstacles that such structures present.

2.4   Market-oriented but..

The last paradox addressed focuses on the desire on the part of the leadership in the Soviet Union to introduce a market-driven orientation into the Soviet economy. Press reports over the last year have chronicled experts from around the world who have visited the Soviet Union to discuss the steps necessary to achieve this transition. **The failed coup and the subsequent steps taken by the republics have ensured that this transition will move forward in some form.**

The paradox in all of this is that such a transition requires a fundamental re-orientation for the entire society and that many people are ill-prepared to make this transition. As one journalist from *The Wall Street Journal* recently noted, "the word market has no equivalent in the Russian language".. and .."some Soviet managers are even hazy about the meaning of profits."[8] Supporting this perspective are statements by such individuals as the chairman of the Central Council of Trade Unions in the Soviet Union who commented, "we know more about space research than we do about market research."[9]

In recent discussions with Soviet business people, we have found that they have recognized the importance of profit motivation as a concept, but only emerging is the understanding of what its implications are. Most Soviet business people we have worked with since *glasnost* (openness) was introduced have focused on how to create momentum for, and participate in the changes taking place in the Soviet Union and have shown little concern for personal gain either for the enterprise or for the themselves.

While certainly this will change as other aspects of the economy develop, ***business people establishing relationships in the Soviet Union should come prepared to discuss how***

---

[8] Peter Gumbel, "Western Money, Technology, Fall on Infertile Soviet Soil," *The Wall Street Journal*, December 1, 1989, p.16.

[9] Ibid, M.N. Rajan and J.L. Graham.

their company can assist Soviet society in making the transition. Profit should be defined as profit for the whole and should necessarily be measured in monetary terms. Polaroid hopes to build its position and profits in the Soviet Union by providing what the nation wants and needs: new jobs, new skills, and some exports.[10]

2.5 Tips for Managers Doing Business

Mahesh N. Rajan and John L. Graham in a recent *California Management Review* article titled "Nobody's Grandfather was a Merchant: Understanding the Soviet Commercial Negotiation Process and Style" suggested the following tips for managers doing business in the Soviet Union.

1) Be Cautious

While changes are taking place at a rapid pace and there are enormous opportunities for businesses in the Russian marketplace, it is still a political as well as an economic situation. Politics can overrule economics. Investing in such an environment can be perilous and the dangers should be recognized.

However, Rajan and Graham's advice should be taken with the recognition that business does go on in a multitude of political environments.

---

[10] *New York Times*, September 1, 1991, p.6.

The New York Times, within a few days of the coup noted in a front page article that business dealings in many ways are apolitical and were continuing even as the coup unfolded.

2) Be Open-minded

Nations around the world have long standing perceptions of the Soviet Union. These biases can hinder objective evaluations and lead to misunderstandings based on the old realities rather than the new realities. Countries and companies that make a more objective assessment of where the country is going, and the hurdles it must overcome to get there, will be in a better position to build and participate in a long term relationship.

3) Be Culturally Sensitive

The Soviet people are a proud and committed people and because of their culture and history, they are traditionally suspicious of outsiders. They appreciate foreigners who have taken the time to develop an awareness of their historical and cultural roots

4) Be Patient

Many of the roles which are part of any international business venture are being filled by relative newcomers to the process. *Since 1988,*

over 5,000 Soviet companies have applied for the right to negotiate with companies outside of the Soviet Union. This number is sure to increase as progress is made toward democracy. As a result, many of the Russian business people participating in these activities are relatively new to the process. Foreign business managers demonstrating an understanding of both the situation and the participants in a business deal can lay a firmer foundation for future business dealings.

5) Exchange Views about Negotiation Processes

Managers should not assume that the negotiation process which they use in their own country is the only right way to negotiate establish a business relationship. Rather managers should start by asking how the process works in Russia and then position their own approach as the way things are done in their country. With this as a base, negotiations can proceed form mutual understanding and respect of alternative processes.

6) Be Flexible

Foreign managers need to demonstrate flexibility and a willingness to explore other options during the negotiation process and beyond. This is especially true in the area of countertrade.

Tambrands, a New York-based maker of feminine hygiene supplies exports Soviet cotton and uses the hard currency from these sales as a way to repatriate profits. While many American companies have rejected countertrade as a form of payment, with over 20% of world trade financed through this method, many American firms may need to reconsider their position.

7) Have a Long-Term Orientation

Alfred Herrhausen, Former CEO of Germany's biggest bank, Deutsche Bank, recently noted that the current transition "will take at least two generations. One generation is necessary to be willing to introduce freedom, but it will be the next to figure out how to make economic use of its benefits." **Korea's Daewoo recently gave a Soviet ministry 50 automobiles - a $250,000 investment toward future sales and goodwill.**

Examples such as these illustrate that many firms from around the world recognize the importance of this marketplace for both the near term and the long term. Companies with shorter term expectations will be at a potential disadvantage to those who are willing to wait for the long run benefits to be realized.

Getting Started

Sweeping changes have created paradoxes that affect business relationships.

- Soviet business people are relationship oriented but their negotiating style can be seen as uncompromising and manipulative
- Soviets are eager to embrace capitalism but distrust it
- Soviets reject centralized bureaucracy but recognize that much of what works in the republics is based on a centralized system of control, and there is no ready substitute

Soviets want to be market-oriented but the transition is awkward, difficult, and will take time.

Tips for managers doing business in the Soviet Union

- be cautious
- be open-minded
- be culturally sensitive
- be patient
- exchange views about the negotiation process
- be flexible
- have a long term orientation

SECTION 3

ESTABLISHING A
FOREIGN BUSINESS IN RUSSIA

3.1 Inofirm Businesses

For several years the USSR's attitude toward the establishment of foreign businesses within its borders has been becoming more liberal. *In the USSR, the term "inofirm" refers to a non-Soviet parent organization, frequently multinational in scope, which establishes a business relationship in Russia.* For our purposes then, the term "inofirm business" is used to designate a business established in the Soviet Union by a foreign company, an inofirm. The business relationship, including joint ventures (JVs), inofirm subsidiaries, and other forms of cooperative ventures are frequently referred to by Russians as "representations".

The government has set up the following procedures for establishing and operating foreign firms, banks and organizations:

1) Depending of the nature of their business activities, foreign firms, banks, and organizations may open businesses in USSR when authorized by the appropriate Accrediting Boards: the Ministry

for Foreign Economic Relations; the State Committee for Science and Technology; the Ministry of Civil Aviation; the Merchant Marine; the Ministry of Fisheries; the State Bank of the USSR; the Chamber of Commerce and Industry; the Cabinets of Ministers of the individual Union-Republics, or by the Ministries and Departments in each of the Union-Republics. The Accrediting Bodies also process requests for the establishment of inofirm branch offices or joint ventures among several inofirms. Authorizations by these bodies includes those granted by inter-governmental agreements between the USSR and other national governments.

2) The authorization to establish inofirm businesses will be granted to those inofirms whose cooperation is of interest to Soviet organizations, primarily to

  a) businesses that are already well-known in their own countries or in the world market, especially those with a positive history as a partner to a Soviet organization in a variety of fields of cooperation and those who have concluded large-scale commercial deals with Soviet organizations;
  b) industries that cooperate with Soviet enterprises, organizations, and the Trade Chambers;

c) Associations, Enterprises, and Unions interested in developing trade and economic ties with the Russian Republic;

d) scientific and technical entities that have concluded significant cooperative agreements with corresponding Soviet organizations.

3) Inofirm businesses can be established for the purpose of:

a) performing cooperative agreements in the fields of trade, finance, economics, science and technology, transportation, tourism, and other fields;

b) generating the means for further economic development;

c) deepening and perfecting cooperative ventures;

d) promoting economic, commercial, and scientific/technical, informational and developmental ties with Soviet organizations;

e) enhancing commerce and the fulfillment of investment opportunities;

f) assisting Soviet organizations in developing an export trade in mechanical equipment and other goods and services;

g) importing up-to-date machinery, equipment and technical services;

h) familiarizing Soviet organizations with

the latest achievements in technology as they are developed world-wide.

4) Inofirm businesses are established for the period necessary to accomplish their purposes, but, as a rule, this period will not exceed three years. If at the end of that time the purpose of the inofirm business has not been accomplished in full and an extension of the time-limit would allow for expeditious completion, an application for the extension of the three-year period may be made by applying to the appropriate Accrediting Body.

5) *The inofirm interested in establishing a business within the USSR files a written application with the appropriate Accrediting Body, in which it specifies its purposes and goals. This application and all required attachments must be translated into Russian.* A description of the inofirm's proposed activities, including detailed information on business ties with Soviet organizations, and agreements or commercial transactions concluded with Soviet entities, is submitted. The description of these activities includes the subject, scope and term of the agreement and should address the question of how the inofirm will assist or cooperate in the development of Soviet organizations and entities.

Official documents including the Statutes of

the inofirm business (i.e. Articles of Incorporation), the appropriate extraction from the Trade Register, the appropriate extraction from the Bank Register or other documentation authorizing banking activity are notarized and attached to the application. Further verification must be made, according to existing procedures, by the USSR Consuls abroad. If, according to the country of origin, the authorization of special governmental bodies is necessary for the establishment of the business, then a copy of such authorization verified according to the existing procedures, is also to be attached to the application.

Along with the required application and documents, an inofirm business may be asked by the appropriate Accrediting Body for additional information or documents concerning its activities (i.e.: the audited financial statements of the inofirm, an introductory letter from the bank which serves the inofirm business, etc.)

The inofirm business shall pay an application fee or "stamp duty" for obtaining authorization to establish or prolong the term of its inofirm business in the USSR according to the relevant legislation.

6) The official representative of the inofirm conducting negotiations with the Accrediting Body to establish a business in the USSR on behalf of the inofirm must have Power of Attorney.

7) The authorization for opening an inofirm business is issued by the appropriate accrediting body incorporating the following information:

a) the purpose for the inofirm business to be established;
b) the conditions under which the inofirm business is authorized to open;
c) the term for which the authorization is issued;
d) the number of non-Soviet nationals to be employed in the inofirm business.

8) The provision of the inofirm business's office, living premises for employees, phone, telex communications, and other business and residential services is carried out in Moscow through the Chief Production Commercial Administration for the Diplomatic Corps services at the Ministry for Foreign Affairs (GlavUpDk). It is also carried out through the USSR Chamber of Commerce and Industry. In other USSR cities, this provision is carried out through the corresponding Executive Committees of the City Councils of Peoples Deputies and also by the corresponding organizations of the USSR Chamber of Commerce and Industry.

Employment of Soviet citizens by the inofirm business is carried out in Moscow through the GlavUpDk, and in other cities through the corresponding Executive committees of the City Councils of Peoples Deputies.

9) The inofirm business is considered to be open on the date that the authorization is issued. The authorization becomes invalid if the inofirm does not open the business within six months of the date of the authorization.

1 0) The inofirm business is empowered to act on behalf of the firm or firms it represents if the names of these firms are indicated in its official authorization and the inofirm business is acting in accordance with Soviet legislation.

The inofirm may carry out the functions connected with its services in the USSR for other firms only with the consent of the accrediting body that issued the authorization for the inofirm business to be established. The inofirm business reports to the Ministry of Finance about the financial results of business activity according to an established procedure. These procedures are subject to change and the appropriate process and format should be identified at the time of the reporting.

1 1) Once established, the local head of the inofirm business, based on the officially regis-

tered Power of Attorney, is authorized to act for the inofirm business.

12) Accreditation of the inofirm business's employees is performed by the accrediting body that issued its original authorization within the limits of the permitted number of employees.

13) The Head of the inofirm business:

a) notifies the Ministry of Finance of the USSR within one month of its commencement that the business has opened, its location, and the composition of its foreign work force;

b) reports to the appropriate accrediting body about the composition and changes in its work force, and on any other information requested;

c) reports semiannually on its business activities, in written form, to the accrediting body that issued the authorization for the business to be open. The information requested is set up by the corresponding accrediting body.

14) Under the following conditions, the activities of the inofirm business in the USSR will cease:

a) upon the agreed expiration date if the in-

ofirm has not applied for an extension;
b) if the inofirm business is liquidated;
c) if the business is directly provided for by an intergovernmental agreement between the USSR and a foreign state, and the agreement expires;
d) the corresponding accrediting body decides that the business has violated the conditions on which the inofirm was granted authorization for opening and conducting business, or if there is an infringement of Soviet legislation;
e) if the inofirm decides to close its business in the USSR.

15) In the cases provided for in point 14, either the appropriate accrediting body or the inofirm business notifies the other of the decision taken. If the inofirm business activities are terminated in the USSR the office and living premises provided for to it must be vacated within three months from the date of such notification.

Foreign firms that open a business in the USSR must remember that if they contract their services with a cooperative, the cooperative is permitted to carry out these services only in Moscow, and on a contract basis, as determined by the Chief Production Commercial Administration for the Diplomatic Corps services at the

Ministry for Foreign Affairs of the USSR.
Cooperatives servicing foreign businesses in other
USSR cities on a contract basis are regulated by
the corresponding Administrations of the
Executive committees of the City Councils of
Peoples Deputies, or the corresponding organiza-
tions in the system of the USSR Chamber of
Commerce and Industry.

3.2 Foreign Investments

In recent years the investment policy of the
USSR has undergone drastic changes.

On October 26th, 1990, the President of the
USSR issued a Decree defining foreign investment
policy:

1) Enterprises with foreign participation
can be established in any form stipulated by the
legislation of the USSR and the Union and
Autonomous Republics. Foreign investors (legal
entities and citizens) may invest within the USSR:

   a) through participation in enterprises orga-
      nized jointly with Soviet legal entities
      and citizens;
   b) by acquiring property, shares, and other
      securities;
   c) by acquiring independently, or jointly
      with Soviet legal entities and citizens

the rights to use land, and other proprietary rights including the rights to a long
term lease in compliance with the legislation of the USSR and to the Union and
Autonomous Republics.

2) Investors (legal entities and citizens)
may establish enterprises within the USSR with
100% foreign investment. Under Soviet law this
kind of enterprise is considered a legal entity (a
sample Agreement of Representation for an inofirm wishing to appoint a Russian representative
or agent is included as Appendix 1).

3) Foreign investments within the USSR are
protected and treated equally under the law to
Soviet enterprises, organizations and citizens.

4) The income obtained in the USSR in Soviet
currency by foreign investors may be freely rein-
vested and used in the USSR in compliance with
USSR and Union Republic legislation. This income
may also be remitted abroad in line with existing
policies and laws.

5) In the hope of attracting joint entrepreneurial activities with foreign investors,
joint entrepreneurship zones may be established
in selected areas of the USSR.

The order of economic activities performed

by Soviet enterprises and enterprises with foreign investments, as well as the privileges provided for them within every such zone are set up by the legislation of the USSR, Union and Autonomous Republics, and the appropriate Soviet Peoples Deputies within their domain.

3.3 Legal Foundations for Investments Activities Act

As of January 1st, 1991, the "Legal Foundations for Investments Activities Act" has defined the general legal, and economic, conditions for investment activities in the USSR. It is aimed at assuring equal protection of rights, interest, properties, and other activities independent of effective functioning of market conditions.

The USSR Supreme Council has adopted a similar position and has established a unified legal routine of economic activities in the USSR for foreign and Soviet investors. It also entitles the Republics, with no consent of the central government, to enter into additional agreements concerning the terms of foreign investments invitation.

The Act stipulates the creation of an ad hoc Union-Republican body to develop and carry out a unified policy for the Union territory applying to the invitation of foreign investments.

These foundations set up a national routine for foreign investments. This means that foreign enterprises have the very same investment and business conditions as Soviet enterprises.

The Act does not restrict the spheres of investment. Foreign investors may invest capital in the USSR in every sphere of the economy and carry out any type of economic activity allowed by the laws of the USSR, and the Republics. Foreign capital may be invested throughout the USSR with the authorization of the corresponding Republic's government. Restrictions on foreign investment may be imposed only for National security reasons, and to protect the environment.

Foreign firms may invest capital in the USSR economy by establishing JVs with the Soviet partners, and establishing businesses with 100% foreign capital. Inofirms in the USSR also have the right;

- to purchase property;
- to purchase shares and securities;
- to use land;
- to take up tenancy, and;
- obtain concessions for the development of natural resources.

This Act grants guarantees to foreign investors for the remittance abroad of their income in foreign currency, and the restoration of their share of the property value of the enterprise if activities stop or, if the governing laws change. However, there is no statement within the Act that clarifies under what concrete instances enterprises with the foreign investment may liquidate.

According to specialists one of the Act's faults is the absence of a clause guaranteeing the fulfillment of contracts. This causes a substantial obstacle for the attraction of the foreign firms to joint activities with Soviet organizations.

This Act substantially extends the Republic's rights. They are granted the right to alter the terms of enterprises with foreign participation, and to grant exemption from the Republic's taxes. The Republics economic branches may also define the priorities for foreign investment.

This act also provides for the establishment of a special All-Union body with representatives from every Republic that should coordinate, but not control, as far as is feasible a unified policy on the initiation of foreign investments.

Most experts have a very positive opinion of the adopted Act.

3.4 Commercial Rate of the Ruble

In November of 1990 the commercial rate of the ruble was introduced in the world market at the rate of 1.8 rubles for 1$US. The commercial rate of foreign currency in relation to the ruble was established by the State Bank of the USSR for use in all settlements of foreign trade, and foreign investment in the territory of the USSR. This rate also applies to Soviet investments abroad, and settlements of non-trade character implemented by legal entities. The purchase and sale of foreign currency in the USSR according to market conditions is regulated separately.

The State Bank of the USSR is authorized to correct the commercial ruble rate depending on the change in value of the currency of the leading capitalist countries, or for other reasons. The State Bank may also specify the regulations concerning the application of the ruble commercial rate in specific kinds of settlements.

During the period 1990-91 a number of legislative acts affecting the prices of foreign deliveries were established. These acts include:

1) On November 2nd, 1990 the USSR President decreed "the special procedure for the usage of hard currency in 1991", and issued, based

on this decree, the Resolution of December 8th, 1990 was issued by the Cabinet of Ministers of the USSR. This resolution stipulates the compulsory sale of 40% of the hard currency proceeds to the Vnesheconombank. Thirty percent to seventy percent of the remaining proceeds should be directed to the enterprise's hard currency funds. The rest should be sold to the Union-Republican hard currency fund.

2) The Resolution of the USSR Cabinet of Ministers on January 10th, 1991, enforces import taxes on Soviet enterprises. Tax rates of the main goods groups vary from 100% to 600%.

3) In April of 1991, the hard currency auction of the Vnesheconombank was liquidated, and replaced by the Hard Currency Exchange. The USSR GOSBANK has approved the new "Regulations on Interbank Hard Currency Transactions Performed at the USSR GOSBANK".

These regulations stipulate:

a) bids for hard currency purchase or sale at the Exchange of less then 10,000 $US are not accepted;
b) the GOSBANK has the right to arbitrarily remove from tender bids to purchase hard currency purchased to pay for imported computers, cars and consumer goods.

In the future the above facts may reduce the number of potential customers and lead to a situation in which only a select number of wholesale purchasers of office equipment and computers are able to resell them for rubles in the Soviet marketplace.

A different situation is emerging in the consumer goods field today. With rapid inflation, and low level salaries in the USSR many enterprises are being forced to purchase hard currency to give extra bonuses in the form of consumer goods to their employees. For this reason, consumer goods are considered good opportunities for investment, within the USSR.

One should note that most organizations purchasing consumer goods, purchase only for their employees, and consequently, purchase small lots. A very convenient form of cooperation with Soviet organizations could be barter deals, but to obtain the authorization to trade with barter is very complicated. One practical way to get around this difficulty, is an agreement between the Soviet and the foreign firm to deliver goods at prices several times lower than those on the market. Deals between JVs and middlemen are widespread in the USSR. *Joint ventures are given a number of privileges, and in particular, are exempt from the obligatory sale to the State of 40% of the hard currency proceeds.*

3.5 Hard Currency Transaction Regulation

The "Basic Regulations on Hard Currency Transactions in the USSR" have been established by the GOSBANK of the USSR in compliance with the "Act on Hard Currency Regulation" which principally provides for the new Soviet market rules of hard currency regulation.

This document defines the procedure for foreign firms ruble accounts with Soviet banks. It prohibits some forms of hard currency accounts between Soviet enterprises, and it establishes the provisions for foreign firms to open ruble accounts in the USSR. This document also stipulates new rules for the sale of hard currency, the procedure for importing hard currency into the USSR, and its exchange into rubles by foreign citizens. These provisions have never before been present in the Soviet legislation.

Commercial banks may carry out transactions in hard currency only if they are licensed by the GOSBANK, or by the Central banks of the Republics. Hard currency transactions may be conducted only through authorized banks.

The law stipulates, "Payment in rubles, rendering of services, or concession of any proprietary value in the USSR for hard currency or its equivalent abroad" is prohibited. Also prohibited is "receiving rubles as payment for hard currency transactions, for rendered services, or the concession of any proprietary values abroad"

This means that it is prohibited to transfer hard currency through commercial banks that up till now have been used quite widely by Soviet state enterprises, JVs, Cooperatives, and small enterprises. The substance of hard currency transfer in bank transactions is that the contracting parties do not conduct hard currency exchange, but simply pay for each other's expenses in their own country.

3.6 Trade and Services For The Convertible Currency

A single system has been created to develop trade and services for convertible currency in the USSR. This system includes:

a) an All Union foreign economic association called a "Trade House";
b) an All Union Foreign Economic Association for Consumer Co-operation;
c) trade houses in the Union and Autonomous republics and regions;
d) a network of specialized enterprises and stores.

Joint enterprises may also enter this network as members of associations who participate with foreign legal entities and citizens, and specialize in trade and services for the convertible currency, and the currency equated with it within the USSR in accordance with the permission of the Cabinet of Ministers of the Union and Autonomous republics (or by the authorization of the republican bodies of the state administration).

The sale of goods and services in the USSR for the convertible currency and the currency equated to it, are treated as export operations, and accordingly, the appropriate measures of state regulation of foreign economic activities are applied. This includes registering the trade houses, specialized enterprises, and stores with the Ministry of Economic Connections of the USSR and the Vnesheconombank of the USSR.

The functions of the trade houses defined by the Government are:

a) to render assistance in the organization of joint enterprises with the participation of foreign legal entities and citizens that manufacture goods from imported components, and sell the completed products for the convertible currency and the currency equated to it, as well as maintenance and repair of these products;

    b) to purchase goods at their own expense for commission (consignment);

    c) to perform the mediation functions of production for enterprises in the territories of the republics (regions), and acquisition of products and goods at their own expense.

The retail prices in the convertible currency and the currency equated with it are established by:

    a) the price level for identical goods and services of foreign firms in the retail network abroad;

    b) the customs duties paid in convertible currency if the goods were imported into the USSR;

    c) the quality of the goods and services, and

    d) the home market conditions.

Getting Started

A positive history of cooperation with Soviet organizations or a demonstrated commitment to Soviet economic progress can be important in being allowed to establish an inofirm business in the Soviet Union.

A written application in Russian that specifies the purpose, conditions, terms, and number of non-Soviet employees for the business, as well as other official documents needs to be submitted to the appropriate accrediting body.

Once established

- the inofirm business acts on behalf of the firm it represents
- it reports on its business activities to the Ministry of Finance and its accrediting body
- the inofirm business ceases to exist if its agreed upon term expires, or if it violates its agreement

Foreign Investment Policy stipulates

- foreign investors may invest in any sphere of the economy within the Soviet Union in property, shares and securities; by participating with Soviet legal entities and citi-

zens; or by establishing enterprises with 100% foreign investment and ownership
- investments are protected by the law and the income obtained may be remitted abroad

Legislative acts that affect the prices of foreign deliveries include

- state regulation of the commercial ruble rate
- the sale of 40% of the hard currency proceeds to the state bank (JVs are exempt from this); 30%-70% of the remaining proceeds are directed to the enterprises hard currency funds. The rest is sold to the Union-Republican hard currency fund.
- import taxes on the main goods is from 100%-600%
- replacement of the Hard Currency Auction of the State Bank by the Hard Currency Exchange
    - bids must exceed $10,000
    - the GOSBANK may refuse bids

The basic regulations on hard currency transactions in the USSR allows foreign firms to open public accounts..

Trade houses are useful when organizing JVs. They will also purchase goods on commission.

SECTION 4

ESTABLISHING AND OPERATING
JOINT VENTURES IN THE USSR TERRITORY

Generally there is a significant tax benefit for the Russian firm when they participate in a joint venture with a foreign company if the foreign company has at least 30% ownership. Joint ventures are legal enterprises of any organizational form with foreign participation. In the "Legislative foundations on foreign investments in the USSR" JVs are established as joint stock companies, economic societies, or partnerships with the participation of Soviet and Foreign legal entities and citizens. (See Section 4.1 and Appendix 2 for further information on tax considerations)

If an inofirm negotiates for the establishment of a joint venture in partnership with a Russian organization, it is necessary to discuss the following information at the negotiation stage:

1) The requirements of technical standards and quality of the Joint Venture products (JV).

2) The volume of products to be delivered to the USSR domestic market and abroad.

3) The amount and structure of contribution to the Joint Venture Statutory fund, i.e., to specify exactly what the Soviet party contribution should be composed of. As a rule, it should be a facility (i,e, plant and equipment), not just complex production means (i.e. engineering designs).

4) The material and technical supplies imported by the JV and moved through the wholesale trade network, and industries supply system.

5) A definition of non-Soviet options to use the trade shops, trade marks, and advertising services for the finished products outside of the USSR.

6) A definition of non-Soviet contribution amounts and its structure.(equipment, hard currency funds, technology).

Stipulate the conditions of non-Soviet specialists enlistment and payment, and the JV contract validity terms, and liquidation procedures thereof.

When, in the course of negotiations, suggestions have been laid out according to the points given above, and a concrete compromise has been defined, a "Protocol of Intention" should be signed. It should be based upon the decisions made and should be understood to be an integral part of the establishment of the JV. The Protocol is not legally binding, but it forms an initial framework for working out the final Establishing documents.

All of the clauses in the Protocol of Intention for the establishment of the Joint Venture should be stipulated in the most general form. Subsequent establishing documents will detail the specifics.

4.1 Establishing Documents

The final stage in the establishment of the Joint Venture is signing the establishing documents and the development of a feasibility study. When creating the establishing documents be sure that all the specifics are spelled out in detail and that the obligations of all the parties to the transaction are specified in writing. The Soviet negotiators will frequently be very concerned about these details and the inofirm business representatives should be equally concerned. Such caution at this stage can protect all parties in the joint venture as the activity proceeds.

These documents include:

a) The Contract or Agreement on the JV Establishment.
b) The Statutes of the JV.
c) The Feasibility Study

The Contract and Statutes are signed by the legal representatives of the Soviet and Foreign founders.

Contracts

There are a number of forms needed by the JVs when creating the establishing contracts. Once developed they are reviewed by the USSR Chamber of Commerce and Industry. They account for the joint venture establishment purposes, its activities, its legal status as a legal entity, the statutory fund structure and amount, the functions and procedures of the Higher, Executive and Control bodies (The Higher body of the JV is the "Board of Directors",the Executive body is the "Director", and the Control body is the "Auditing Commission". These are created by every Joint Venture). The procedure of output distribution, the material-technical supplies, the working conditions of the JV employers, and the Contract term and procedure for its termination is also developed in the establishing contracts.

Statues

The Statutes repeat, in many aspects, the Contract clauses. The only difference is: that the Contract mainly fixes the parties' obligations, i.e., the relationship of the Founders to the Joint

Venture, and their rights with respect to the JV. The Statutes pay more attention to the inner workings of the JV - to the Board of Directors competence of the JV, to its direction, etc.

It may be expedient not to include detailed regulation in the Contract and Statutes, because the reality of the Joint Venture's activities may be different than expected or change, and later on it would be very complicated to alter the Statutes. Therefore, to allow for change, the wording "Solution of the matters in question is included within the competence of the joint Venture Board of Directors" is used to address the resolution of emerging issues.

Feasibility Report

Presently there is no official document approving the procedure and form of a feasibility report (TEO) for the JV. Mainly it is developed for calculation of the joint venture's effectiveness based upon "The temporary methods for the definition of economic effectiveness of Joint Ventures established in the USSR territory". This was worked out by the All Union Scientific-Research Institute for Foreign Economic Relations at the State Commission for Foreign Economics of the USSR Cabinet of Ministers. These methods provide for a basis to calculate the feasibility report, i.e., the effectiveness calculation includes an explanatory note discussing the details of the effectiveness calculation. Sometimes the effectiveness calculation is made by methods offered by the foreign partner.

Another method, the COMFAR has been elaborated by the United Nations Industrial Development Organization (UNIDO). It is supported by computer software, and facilitates the calculation of any project's feasibility including foreign partner participation.

4.2 Joint Venture Registration

The Joint Venture is established and has legal entity status the moment it registers with the Ministry of Finance of the USSR.

Joint Venture registration is performed by filing an application in writing, and notarized copies of the following documents:

a) The authorization of a higher organization, or of the corresponding Executive Committee of the appropriate cooperatives, for the establishment of the Joint Venture for the Soviet party.
b) The Contract or Agreement of Joint Venture Establishment.
c) The JV Statutes.
d) The Feasibility Report.

The registered Joint Venture is issued a "Certificate of Joint Venture Registration". The registered JVs are entered into a special Register that is maintained by the Ministry of Finance. It is only after registration, that the JV with the above "Certificate", may enter economic relations, sign contracts, open bank accounts, and be registered at the Ministry for Foreign Economic Relations of the USSR (MFER) as a participant in foreign economic relations.

4.3 The Relationship Of The Joint Venture with the Soviet Organization's Founders

After the Joint Venture is registered and has independent legal entity status, it runs its economic life in many ways independently from the Founder (the Soviet joint venture founder), i.e., after registration, the Founder may affect JV activities exclusively through the representatives of the JV Board of Directors. The JV operates based on its commercial interests. If the interests of the founder are not profitable, the course of action that makes profit supersedes the founder's interests.

The relationship of the Joint Venture and the Soviet Founder shall be built exclusively by contract (i.e., the deliveries from the founder to the JV and vice versa shall be recorded in economic contracts). This includes not only the contracts on deliveries, but the transfer of technology, the leasing of the premises, and the carrying out of construction. The JV, as a rule, keeps staffing to a minimum, and for completing large-scale works, may from time to time contract the services of specialists from outside (often from the founder) on a fixed term. The delivery of goods and services is performed on agreed upon prices. Since this type of contract is used rather frequently between the founder and the Joint Venture, they may form a general agreement between them. The General Agreement defines main principles so that repetition is avoided in every new situation.

3.4 Joint Venture Material-Technical Supplies

One of the serious problems facing JVs is that they operate by market principles, and not by the order of the State. This is a problem because the entire material-technical supply system has been built on the basis of a funded resource distribution that is directly coordinated by State orders. Therefore, as early as the authorization from the higher Organization stage of Joint Venture establishment, the Soviet Founder has to make an agreement to introduce the JV into the system of funded supplies, which the higher Organization itself utilizes. Joint Ventures may also explore other possibilities that are available through wholesale trading. In practice when JVs find themselves stranded,they often contact co-operatives seeking barter generally find a way to make a deal.

The following are the GOSSNAB instructions for joint ventures on the channels to be used for acquiring material-technical supplies. In rank order they are:

a) operative supplies channeled through the funds of the Ministries, Departments and Territorial bodies.
b) through wholesale trade.
c) through the purchase of currency for exported goods from Soviet enterprises and organizations.
d) through importation.

Joint Ventures use all of these channels depending on the situation.

4.5 Realization Of Joint Venture Goods And Services In The USSR Domestic Market And Abroad

According to the initial version of the Regulations on Joint Entrepreneurship, Joint Ventures are instructed to operate in the Soviet Union domestic market (to purchase and manufacture any products) only through the OBJEDINENIJA for Foreign Trade, and only for rubles at prices comparable with world market prices.

As far as the JVs' manufacture of products in the external market is concerned, further regulations permit the JVs to acquire the right (in the case of currency shortages) to purchase goods anywhere in the Soviet Union, that could be supplied to the foreign participant by the external market (such as raw materials).

4.6 Financial Issues Related To The Joint Venture's Activities

The main sources of financial activities for JVs are:

a) the monetary resources contributions to the Statutory fund
b) the depreciation charges generated through the JV
c) the reserve fund of the Joint Venture
d) other JV funds assigned for development of science and technology
e) the credit resources

The JVs rubles are deposited in bank accounts opened with local bank branches.

To make international hard currency payments and deposits the Joint Venture needs to open bank accounts with the Vnesheconombank of the USSR or with its branches, or through other authorized financial institutions.

The Soviet JV participant can be granted a credit for making a contribution to the Statutory Fund. Such a credit is granted for 3 years as a rule, and corresponds to the Statutory fund amount. There is no official regulation for the correspondence ratio, but as a rule, the amount of a loan based on this contribution (amount of credit) shall not exceed the Statutory Fund contribution.

4.7 Taxation and Income Allocation

Taxation is performed according to the current regulations of the Ministry of Finance "On Joint Ventures Taxation" and "On Some Partial Alterations of Joint Venture Taxation".

The alteration referred to suspends the exemption of taxes on Joint Ventures for the first 2 years from the declaration of receipt of profit (reflected in the bookkeeping balance).

These regulations are extended to the Joint Venture branch offices, located in the USSR *that are legal entities*.

Taxation is the only way JVs impact the State budget. Payment for the funds and labor resources is not collected from JVs.

4.8 Some Considerations For Recognizing Income And Proceeds

Some things to be considered when recognizing income and proceeds of the Joint Venture and how it is allocated include the following:

1) The difference in the proceeds from the JV products and the cost of the products manufactured (all the expenses that the Joint Venture incurs including management expenses) are totaled in the balance income. From the balance income the charges are made to the reserve fund. The annual amounts of charges are stipulated in the Statutes or Contract that established the Joint Venture (or the Board of Directors establish the annual amount).

2) Contributions to various funds including development funds (to further future research) and reserve funds (to ensure financial stability) are made out of the balance income. Deductions are made to the funds of manufacturing development and science and technology. There may be several funds for these types. There is no limit on the deductions to these development funds. Deductions to the reserve fund can be made until the amount of the fund is 25% of the Statutory Fund for the JV.

3) JVs can also establish funds for material stimulation and collective social development. As with the other funds discussed in point 2, contributions to these funds are made with pretax dollars. There can be a number of such funds: for social development, housing construction, etc. These funds are not regulated, i.e., they can be formed at the JV's discretion.

4) After the deductions for the reserve fund, for the development of science and technology funds, and for other applicable funds have been made, the remaining income is taxable. An average tax rate for the JVs is 30%. There may be privileges for JVs granted in the Far East region. If there are grounds, the JV may also appeal to the finance inspection bodies (which collect the taxes) with a request for suspension or a partial reduction of the tax rate.

5) The Ministry of Finance of the USSR is elaborating now on a differential taxation scale for Joint Ventures which operate in various fields.

6) Thirty percent of the taxable income is paid to the State budget in taxes. The currency of the income does not matter, (in $US or rubles) the taxes on the income is paid off in rubles only.

The remaining income after all deductions to the funds are made, and the taxes due are paid, is called the allocated income. It shall be allocated among the JV Founders in proportion to their contribution to the Statutory Fund (The regulation has been canceled that limits the participation for the foreign partner to 49%). If, in the allocated income there were rubles or other hard currencies, they should be divided in the same manner as any other income.

4.9 Income Due To The Foreign Partner

If all of the income is obtained in hard currency, it can be transferred abroad to the foreign partner (by remittance). The income remitted would be taxed at 20%, which is payable in the remittance currency to the Vnesheconombank. If the foreign partner does not remit the income, but deposits it with the Vnesheconombank, the 20% remittance tax is not due.

When foreign partners accumulate income in rubles, they face a rather complex situation that has not yet been solved. The fact is that many firms cooperating in joint entrepreneurial activities idealistically think that economic reforms will prompt progress, and that it may become possible to invest those rubles into the Soviet peoples economy to gain profit. They are even prepared to purchase Soviet goods with that profit, or to invest it (if the profit is in rubles) as their share in another JV whose products would be sold on the Western market, thereby obtaining the hard currency needed.

These "ruble" means are needed by foreign partners to meet the expenditures of the large scale actions of the Soviet market: to expand trade ties, business trips for their staff, their representation, etc. They use joint ventures in part as businesses based in the Soviet Union.

The regulations concerned with the 20% tax due on the foreign partner's remitted income consider it to be expedient to extend certain privileges on the remittance of the money abroad for certain industries and locales. JVs specializing in the output of consumer goods, of medical instruments, of medication, of science-consumption products of great national-economic value, as well as, enterprises located in the Far East economic region among others are given special considerations. Such considerations should be explored by firms active in these industries or locales once they have made the decision to explore the establishment of a JV in the Soviet Union.

4.10 The Procedure For Establishing Joint Venture Branch Offices And Businesses

A necessary condition for JV branch office establishment is the inclusion of the possibility, and right for its establishment, in the establishing documents of the JV.

A general form of such wording is: "The enterprise may establish branch offices and businesses in the USSR, in the partner country, and in the territories of any third parties".

The branch office functions under the Regulations controlling it. Such Regulations are implemented in compliance with the procedure defined in the Statutes of the JV. The Board of Directors shall establish and adopt the Regulation of the branch office.

It should be indicated whether or not, the branch office is granted legal entity status. If it does have this status it is should be indicated that "the branch office shall not be responsible for the enterprise's obligations, and the enterprise shall not be responsible for the obligations of the branch office".

The branch offices of Joint Ventures established in the USSR are to be registered, as previously mentioned, with the Instruction of the Ministry of Finance of the USSR: "On the Procedure for Joint Venture Registration."

To register branch offices it is necessary to file the following with the Ministry of Finance (details on these were given earlier):

a) an application for registration.
b) notarized copies of the Establishing Documents of the Joint Venture (the Statutes and Contract of the JV).
c) the regulations of the branch office approved by the higher body of the JV.

After registering branch offices, they are entered into a separate Register. Those established abroad are registered in compliance with the country's legislation applying to a firm of that country.

There are no explicit definitions, however, of a branch office. If the branch office is a legal entity, it should have Statutes of its own.

Branch offices established as a legal entity that attract other partners, make the participants part not only of the given JV, but also part of a third firm. In essence it is not a branch office as such, but a new joint venture.

The only reason why branch offices are not considered independent Joint Ventures, is that within the Regulations of branch offices, power is shared between the branch office board of Directors and of the JV's Board of Directors.

Getting   Started

In establishing a joint venture

- negotiate with the foreign partner about
  the general requirements, structures, and
  obligations of the venture.   Record this in a
  "Protocol of Intentions"
- the JV is registered through the authorization of a higher organization using the
  following documents
    - the contract or Agreement of JV
      Establishment
    - the JV Statutes
    - the Feasibility Report

Once established, JVs

- should attempt to acquire their supplies
  and raw materials from within the Soviet
  Union
- explore the use of various funds as part of
  their treatment of taxes

The average tax rate for JVs is 30%. Income remitted abroad is taxed an additional 20%

JVs branch offices are registered similar to JVs.
The possibility of JV branch offices should be
included in the JV establishing documents.

SECTION 5

CUSTOMS REGULATIONS
IN THE USSR

A contemporary organizational-legal system for foreign economic activities in the USSR has been created in recent years through the adoption of Acts, and other regulatory-legal documents. The system of State regulation for foreign economic activities includes:

a) registration of the participants in foreign economic ties;
b) declaration of goods and other types of property transported and transferred over the State borders of the USSR;
c) order of export and import of particular goods in the State general assignments;
d) regulation and measurement of foreign economic ties.

Reforms in the foreign economic activities sphere have created profound changes in the legal basis, forms, and methods of Customs control.

The aim of Customs control is: to reliably secure State interests in the process of production, and other functions of foreign economic ties, to effectively implement the Customs tariffs of the USSR, and also to accumulate statistical information in a special data bank on USSR Customs.

Introduction of these measures is aimed at the state-legal system established for participants in foreign economic activities. The state-legal system can accelerate and facilitate the formalities of cargoes through Customs on the basis of internationalization, and Customs procedures unification. It can also be of great help with Customs documentation. One such innovation in Customs widely practiced abroad is a unified document for daily use by Soviet State Customs control bodies:

  a) to declare cargo,
  b) set up the order for the transportation of goods, and
  c) to declare the property of participants in foreign economic ties.

5.1 Savings Mechanisms On Tax Payments And Custom House Duties

Frequently for purposes of export and import in cooperative arrangements between Russian firms and foreign businesses, there is not a standard basis for agreeing on the value of certain types of semi-finished products and products of non-completed production. The partners are permitted to establish the agreed export-import prices to limit the amount of taxes due. *Customs duties on cooperative supplies for production (raw materials and semi-finished goods) are on average 2-3 times lower than customs duties on finished items.*

Cooperation between Russian firms and foreign firms in production is particularly effective in reducing import taxes and duties on the import of durable consumer goods to the Soviet market. In this case it is sufficient to remove, for example, sewing machine casings from their "inner parts", and declare the imported goods part of a cooperative production, to reduce the import duties and taxes by almost 3 times.

5.2 Terms And Language Of Customs Transactions

Before the description of the list of goods it is necessary to explain the terms being used in Customs practice:

goods - articles transmitted over the border that are objects of foreign trade, purchase, sale, or exchange (barter);

property - articles transported over the USSR border belonging to enterprises, associations, organizations that are not objects of foreign trade or exchange (barter). For example, gifts, exhibition property, specimens, articles imported into the USSR or exported from the USSR on a temporary basis, and so on;

declarant - the enterprises, associations, and organizations declaring goods and property to Customs;

declarant's commissioner - a person provided by the declarant with the powers of declaring. The documents conferring such power is procured by the organization in writing or by order of the organization-declarant;

consignment - goods or property sent to a single consignor according to a single transportation document (a waybill, of lading, etc.), according to the transportation rules, and consigned at one mail bill, or transported in hand luggage by a single person making their way over the USSR border. The goods and property consigned on one occasion only, by one consignor, at one railroad station, independent of the waybill number, to a single consignee address at another station is regarded one consignment;

order supplies - supplies of goods for sale or exchange, that will cross the border at an undetermined time for foreign purchase, sale, or exchange, excluding supplies regulated by international Agreements of the USSR on commodity turnover and payment.

customs regulations - are established according to the nature and purpose of the goods or property transported across the USSR border, and according to the customs procedures applied to the article in question.

customs procedures - carries out the control of goods and property transported across the USSR border. This procedure includes customs examination, registration of official documentation, checking customs cargo declaration, accepting payment, accumulating statistical data for the USSR GOSCOMSTAT, and other actions performed by the State customs control bodies of the USSR in accordance with USSR legislation on Customs regulation issues.

5.3 Some Considerations For Exporting And Importing Goods And Property

Some things to be considered when filing a request to import and export goods and property include:

1) The enterprise, association, or organization must be registered as a foreign economic relations participator with the Ministry for Foreign Economic Relations.

2) Licenses need not be requested for the manufactured products of Joint Ventures, or for the goods imported by international associations and organizations into the USSR for their own consumption.

3) If a license is needed it must be presented to the appropriate Customs institution.

Licenses authorize foreign economic transactions of the import or export of certain goods by competent State bodies. They can be for one occasion or for a fixed term.

Licenses should be obtained if the goods exported from or imported to the USSR are:

a) general purpose goods of the State included in lists approved by the USSR Cabinet of Ministers;
b) import-export goods restricted for set periods of time according to separate groups of goods;
c) from countries or groups of countries limited by quotas;
d) goods to which a license has been extended.

Licenses are granted:

a) for goods that are State general purpose

goods: assigned by the Ministries and Departments of the USSR, and by the Union Republics Cabinet of Ministers;
b) for goods subjected to export and import restrictions by the USSR Ministry for Foreign Economic Relations.

4) Licenses should cover imported goods used by the participant involved in foreign economic ties or for manufacture and export.

5) Authorization should be obtained and documentation of this authorization be provided for the Customs institutions or other State bodies controlling the particular commodity.

Refer to the following institutions for authorization:

a) the State Commission on Food and Purchases - for products of plant and animal origin;
b) the USSR Ministry of Health Institutions - for medicine and sources of toxic radiation;
c) the USSR Ministry of Interior Bodies - for arms, ammunition and highly effective poisons;
d) the USSR Ministry of Communications - for radio, electronics, and high frequency facilities;

e) the USSR Ministry of Culture Institutions - for the export of cultural activities abroad;
f) the USSR State Committee on Science and Technology - for the export of Soviet inventions and another of scientific-technological activities or achievements.

Buying goods for resale in the domestic market is not permitted unless it is provided for by current regulations.

It is necessary for joint ventures, international associations and organizations to be authorized by the USSR Ministry for Foreign Economic Relations (MFER) to carry out middleman transactions. Production Co-operatives may not carry out middleman transactions.

If the goods transported across the border are being exchanged as barter, additional documentation confirming authorization of the deal is required.

Authorizations for barter deals are granted:

a) by the USSR Cabinet of Ministers;
b) by the State Commission for Foreign Economy-for transactions with total values up to 5 million rubles.

Individual USSR Ministries and Departments in agreement with the USSR MFER may process transactions of their subordinate enterprises, associations and organizations on buying raw, and initial materials, or equipment for output, or commodities for peoples' consumption.

It is not necessary to obtain authorization on barter transactions performed: for enterprises and organizations of the USSR Ministry for Trade-for goods consumed by people out of the provided marketing fund, for the USSR State Committee for Material-Technical Supplies-for distributed production of manufacturing-technical goods, or under USSR International Treaties in which such transactions have been stipulated.

Enterprises, associations and organizations have to carry out the same requests for the passage of property, as for goods.

Property may be imported to, or exported from the USSR on a temporary basis. Temporary imports and exports may cross the border on the condition that they are re-imported or re-exported within one year from the date of crossing the border.

Allowed to cross the border are reasonable quantities of:

a) property being passed over at no payment basis;
b) advertising materials and souvenirs;
c) food imported to the USSR for inofirm purposes;
d) food imported to the USSR to exhibit in the USSR (exhibitions, contests, congresses, symposia, seminars, fairs, and all other events of this type);
e) food imported to the USSR, as well other items of personal use to the foreign staff contracted to work within the USSR.

Customs procedures for property aimed at rendering assistance in times of natural calamities, military clashes, technological catastrophes and accidents, or transportation wrecks may be performed after they cross the USSR border, but not later than one month from the date of passage.

Foreign goods may be transported across the USSR territory, as long as their importation to, and transportation within the USSR is not prohibited.

Declaration of goods and property is performed by registering, and declaring the cargo to customs according to an established form.

A cargo customs declaration consists of four stitched sheets and are completed for each lot of goods or property on the condition that the goods in the lot are the same. Should a lot of goods or property include several names or categories additional sheets are to be used.

Currently, the largest organization carrying out declarations is the VVO "Sojuzvneshtrans". Payment for performance of Customs procedures is collected in different ways depending on who is transporting the goods or property over the USSR border.

5.4 Penalties For Customs Violations

There are regulations for making way and declaring goods and property transported over the State border. They reflect current Soviet norms of responsibility. These norms in aggregate with the Customs Code of the USSR provide the legal basis for the penalties implemented to infringers.

The infringing declarants may be subjected to the following penalties:

1) Suspension of shipment if the cargo is declared incorrectly, if it fails to provide the necessary grounds for crossing the border, for non-payment of customs duties and fees, or other infringements.

2) Seizure of the imported goods and property by the State may occur if:

a) the importer fails to eliminate the infringements revealed in the course of declaration, or refuses to return the goods or property to the Customs institutions abroad within a month (7 days for perishables);

b) the importer fails to declare all the information concerning the imported articles that should be declared or represented to Customs;

c) the articles are not transported under the importer's true name (in the latter two cases a charge of smuggling is filed with the court against those involved).

3) A compulsory recovering of duties and/or property on temporarily imported property if the property can no longer be called temporary.

4) Loss of license to do business for a term of up to 6 months for participants in foreign activities who non-faithfully compete, or cause damage to State interests.

5) Suspension of foreign economic transactions, or the particular transaction, for a term of up to 1 year for the repeated failure by the declarant to comply with their obligations of timely payment for Customs procedures.

Customs institutions may impose monetary fines upon persons responsible for facts revealed in the course of declaration that show damage, destruction or loss to Customs, and any other deeds infringing Customs regulations.

In conclusion, it is worth noting that any Customs institution's decision concerning cases of Customs law infringements can be appealed by the persons involved to a higher Customs institution or, according to legal procedures in compliance to the USSR Customs Code.

Getting Started

The state regulation for foreign economic ties in customs control includes

- registration
- declaration of goods
- order of export and import
- regulation of foreign economic ties

Customs duties on cooperative supplies for production are 2-3 times lower than those for finished goods.

The enterprise, association, or organization must be registered as a foreign economic relations partner to export or import goods.

Businesses conducting "middleman" transactions must be authorized by the MFER.

The penalties for customs violations are suspension and seizure of the imported goods, suspension or loss of license to do business, or monetary fines. Customs institution decisions can be appealed.

APPENDICES

Appendix 1

Sample Agreement On Representation (Agency Agreement)

1. We entrust to you the exclusive right to sell our manufactured goods in the territory _____
_____hereinafter referred to as the Representation territory.

The scope of the present Agreement is limited by the above commercial spheres. Should you become a middleman in another type of commercial deal, it must be covered by additional conditions concerning commission remuneration.

2. You pledge to represent our society's interests (firm, enterprise, etc.) in good faith, not to represent any competing firms, and not to sell their products for this agreement to be valid. The present agreement may be terminated if there is any infringement of these clauses by registered letter.

You pledge to follow all of our instructions and orders concerning your business activities. You pledge also to keep confidential our commercial secrets and conditions offered to you after the expiration of the present Agreement.

3. Deals that you mediate should only be regarded final with our confirmation by letter or telex.

Itemized accounts shall be charged by us. Cashing accounts shall be carried out only by us.

4. Commercial correspondence with clients shall be performed by us directly. You shall transmit the letters to us as appropriate.

Should there be correspondence directly between you and clients within the Representation territory, you are to transmit copies of the correspondence to us. You bear the responsibility for identifying the firm representation. The name of the firm representation is_____
_____.

5. At least once a month you are to send us written reports on the market (about the deals, the right for conclusion of which has been afforded to you by p. 1 of the present Agreement) and also about the price dynamics in the territory where you represent our firm.

6. You are expected to initiate deals within the territory you represent our interests, to support us at the deal's conclusion, and especially, to render assistance with payment.

7. We pledge to pay you during the term of the Agreement commission on the net income for all contracted deals.

When you request goods for the territory you represent our firm in, we shall calculate our prices based on the corresponding freight costs, and the state of the market.

Should you, on that basis, obtain a higher price, the difference is to be divided between us equally. However, if we cut prices for you, and you later manage to receive higher prices on the discounted goods, we will not divide the profit between us. Increasing prices on this basis would be defined separately based on the state of the market.

Commission shall be paid exclusively for the period of payment receipts against our bills according to the amounts entered from the clients. The commission calculation and payment for the quarter shall be performed by the end of the quarter with no payment of interest for the period.

Compensation for general (overhead) expenses (expenses of mail, for sending of cables, telexes, business trips and so on) and expenses paid in cash shall not be covered.

8. All alternations to the present Agreement shall

be valid only in writing.

9. The present Agreement shall be effected on
_____, and shall be valid up to
_____. No notifications of its termination are given at this time.

Both parties reserve the right to cancel the present Agreement by mailing a registered letter if there is any infringement of the present Agreement conditions. The cancellation takes effect immediately.

10. Should one, or several clauses of the present Agreement due to any reason become invalid all other clauses remain intact.

11. The present Agreement is drawn up on the basis of the _____ law. To construe the Agreement, the law of _____ _____ is implemented. The disputes which may arise shall be resolved in the Court of_____
_____
_____.

Appendix 2

Additional Information On The Tax Privileges For Russian Enterprises With Inofirm Participation

Enterprises with foreign participation pay an income tax on their turnover under both Union and Russian legislation. They also pay export and import taxes, sales tax, and the foreign participants pay income tax. The income tax for both groups is due the moment receipt of income is declared.

Enterprises with foreign participation are divided into two groups depending on the foreign partner share in the Statutory fund. The first group has participation up to 30%, the second over 30%.

The first group's Union income tax is 45%. The second group's income tax is 30%, unless they operate in the Far East region, and then it is 10%. Under Russian legislation, enterprises with foreign participation of the first group pay 35% income tax, and the second group pays 25% income tax.

These tax rates only apply if the profitability norm does not exceed the maximum level set up for Soviet enterprises. Should the maximum profitability levels be exceeded the tax rates provided for all the other enterprises are implemented (see above). These privileges are provided for enterprises operating in the following industries: hydroenergetics, fuel, mining, metallurgy, and the chemical industry. These privileges are also provided to enterprises that sell their production at prices no higher than State prices. The superprofit in excess of the maximum levels in such enterprises is not taxed.

Legal Foundations for Foreign Investments Act

According to the "Legal Foundations for Foreign Investments Act," the superprofit tax would be canceled for all enterprises with foreign participation, and their income tax would be 35% independent of their profitability level.

As of January 1st, 1991, all enterprises with foreign participation, as well as other participators in foreign economic relations are to pay export, import, and the turnover taxes.

The import tax is set up for the 99 different groups of goods (mainly consumer goods), and their tax rates range from 20% to 1300%. Exempt from taxation is production imported into the USSR by firms with foreign partner contribution in the Statutory Fund. Also exempt from taxation on import are goods supplied for charity purposes, goods that are being sold in the USSR for hard currency, and goods that are to be re-exported. Export taxes are set up for 17 groups of goods (which include: raw materials, semi-finished products, fuel, spirits and alcoholic products) and the tax rates range from 5% to 50%.

Turnover tax rates for the JVs are set up for 9 groups of goods (mainly consumer goods) corresponding with the percentage of the turnover in retail prices after the trade abatement and transportation expenses deduction, and are from 10% to 90%.

All Soviet enterprises, as well as those with foreign participation, pay a 5% President Tax on the value of the production realized.

All enterprises with foreign participation pay tax on the foreign participant's income. This tax is paid both to the Russian and Union legislation. The tax on the foreign partner's income and remittance abroad is 15%. The tax is due in the remittance currency.

Under the Russian and Union legislation the tax privileges for enterprises with foreign participation of less than 30% is similar to those provided for enterprises with no foreign participation.

Enterprises with foreign partners who share more than 30% in the Statutory Fund enjoy additional privileges: if they are established in the material production industries (excluding the extracting and fisheries industries), they are exempt from income tax payment for two years (in the Far East - for three years) after they receive the declared profit.

Taxes on enterprises with foreign participation, or 100% foreign capital, are the same as the taxes on JVs with a foreign capital share over 30%.

If the JV has incurred losses, the income directed to cover the losses is tax exempt for 5 years.

Appendix 3

Directory of Agencies

State Ministries

Chamber of Commerce and Industry of USSR
1036484, Moscow
Kuivysheva St., 6
Tel. 923-43-23 (English spoken); 206-77-75

Council of Ministers of RSFSR
103274, Moscow
Krasnopresnenskaya, Naberezhnaya, 2
Tel. 205-43-25 (English spoken)

Industrial Center of Informatics and Electronics
123557, Moscow
Presensky Val, 19
Contact: V. Kleshyov, General Director

Ministry of Culture of USSR
121835, Moscow
Arbat, 35
Tel. 241-07-09

Ministry of Finance of the RSFSR
103381, Moscow
Neglinnaya, 23
Contact: V.E. Klochko
Tel. 200-15-96 (English spoken)
925-58-47; 200-05-57

Ministry of Finance of the USSR
103097, Moscow
Kuivyshdva, 9
Tel. 298-99-92 (English spoken); 298-91-30;
998-98-01

Ministry of Foreign Affairs
121200, Moscow
Smolenskaya-Sennaya Square, 32/34
Tel. 244-41-94 (English spoken); 244-16-06

Ministry of Foreign Economic Connections
121200, Moscow
Smolenskaya-Sennaya Square, 32/34
Tel. 244-29-87 (English spoken); 220-13-50

Ministry of Foreign Affairs of the RSFSR
129110, Moscow
Mira Ave., 49A
Tel. 206-57-60 (English spoken)
Tel. 281-10-11; 971-10-36

Ministry of Trade of the RSFSR
117311, Moscow
Kirova, 47
Tel. 207-70-00

Insurance Companies

Foreign Insurance Board of USSR (Ingosstrakh)
113035, Moscow
Pyatnitzkya, 12
Contact: M.A. Safronov
Tel. 231-16-77

Russian Insurance Board
127254, Moscow
Studjony Pas., 1
Tel. 476-94-71
Telex 411700 (3606) Pta Su Sovinstrakw
Fax 292-65-11 (3606) Sovinstrakw

State Insurance Board (Gosstrakh USSR)
103473, Moscow
Nastasyinsky Pas., 3, Block 2
Contact: V.V. Shahov
Tel. 299-29-42

State Insurance Board (Gosstrakh RSFSR)
103051, Moscow
Neglinnaya, 23
Contact: Y.S. Bugayev
Tel. 200-29-95

Associations

All-Union Self Financing Economic Association of
Chamber of Commerce and Industry of the USSR
"Soyuzregion"
103055, Moscow
2-D Lesnoypas., 10
Contact: V.S. Nicolenko
General Director
Tel. 258-04-16

All Union Self Financing Foreign Economic
Association "Aviaexport"
121351, Moscow
Ivana Franko, 48
Contact: V.T. Klimov
General Director

Association of Business Cooperation with Foreign
Countries "Agropromserbis"
103030, Moscow
Chernyshevsky Per., 4
Contact:G.V. Vartanov
General Director
Tel. 281-22-01; 288-30-05
Telex 411624

Association of Foreign Economic Cooperation
"Prodintern"
121200, Moscow
Smolenskaya-Sennaya Square, 32/34
Tel. 244-29-14
Telex 411206

"Belinterconsalt" (Soviet-American Joint Venture
BELKO SAJV)
Minsk
Contact: D.B. Galyash
Tel. (0172) 34-20-77
Fax (0172) 34-26-78

Foreign Economic Cooperation "Agroporomeexport"
129041, Moscow
B. Pereslavskaya St., 14
Contact: V.V. Nikitin
General Director

Foreign Trade Association "Avtopromimport"
109017, Moscow
Pyatnitzkaya, 50/2
Contact: V.V. Doroteev
General Director
Tel. 231-81-96

International Economic Association for Arranging
Business Cooperation and Equipment Deliveries
103074, Moscow
Kitaysky Pas., 7
Contact: F.Y. Ovchinnikov
Tel. 220-46-04

Moscow Association of Business Cooperation with
Foreign Organizations and Firms
103062, Moscow
Kolpachney Pereulok, 4, Room 54
Tel. 206-90-93
Telex 411297
Contact: V.A. Pospelov
General Director
Tel. 975-12-58

Regional Foreign Economic Association "Voronezh"
39900, Voronezh
Ordzhonikidze St., 25
Contact: M.T. Critinin
Tel. (0732) 55-08-04
Fax (0732) 55-58-08
Telex 153212 Ravor Su

Soviet-American Joint Venture "Intermedbio (IMB)"
117511, Moscow
Leninsky Prospect, 156
Tel. 434-10-20
Telex 411649
Fax 439-10-20
Contact: A.P. Tzelishev
Tel. 433-11-66

Soviet Foreign Trade Society "Sovintersport"
12189, Moscow
B. Rzhevsky Pas., 5
Contact: V.I. Galaev
Tel. 291-91-49
Telex 411578

The USSR Association of Foreign Economic Cooperation for Medium and Small Business, The Production-Creative Union <<D.A.H.C.>>
P.O. Box 30, 2 Tverscaya-Yamscaya Street, 15
125047, Moscow, USSR
Contact: Stanislav V. Tverdohlebov
President
Tel. 209-29-50 (English spoken); 209-29-68; 209-69-76
Telex 411700 <<D.A.H.C.>>
Telefax 292-65-11-<<D.A.H.C.>>

Banks, Credit Organizations, and other Financial Institutions

Autobank of the USSR
101514, Moscow
Lesnaya, 41
Contact: A.L. Mishin
Chairman of the Board
Tel. 258-48-93

Business "Rossiyskaya Conversia"
127018, Moscow
Box 47
Tel. 290-96-51
Telex 411700 "Rosconversia", 3898
Fax 292-65-11 "Rosconversia"
Contact: A. Ckibalchenko
Director

Commercial Bank "Kreditprombank"
Association Russia
129868, Moscow
Mira Ave., 84
Contact: V.L. Tzaregorodtzev
President
Tel. 281-89-36

Commodity Exchange "Conversia"
1040056, Dzerzhinsky,
Moscowskaya Oblast,
Sovjetskaya St., 6
Contact: V. Martynjuk
Commercial Director
Tel. 551-01-88

Gosbank of the USSR
Moscow
Neglinnaya. 12, Block 6
Tel. 921-31-16

International Bank of Economic Cooperation
107815, Moscow
Mash Poryvayevoy St., 11
Contact: V.S. Khokhlov
Chairman of the Board
Tel. 975-38-94; 204-72-20

International Investment Bank
10707, Moscow
Mashy Poryvajevoy, 7
Contact: A.N. Belichenko
Chairman of the Board
Tel. 975-38-25

International Moscow Bank
103009, Moscow
Pushkinskaya St., 5/6
Tel. 292-97-42

Joint-Stock Commercial "Aeroflot"
125167, Moscow
Leningradsky Ave., 37A
Tel. 155-59-51

Magadansky Commercial Bank
685500, Magadan
Proletarskaya, 25/1
Contact: P. Lukjanov
Chairman of the Board
Tel. 207-09-17 (Moscow)
Fax 200-42-45 (Moscow)

Moscowsky Commercial Bank "Finwestbank"
Moscow
Afanasjevsky Pas., 9
Contact: Y. Begman
Chairman of the Board
Tel. 249-07-06

Vnesheconombank of USSR
Moscow
Novokirovsky Ave., 15/31
Tel. 204-61-60

Special Customer Registration Form:

Thank you for your recent purchase. If you are interested in ordering additional copies of this book or notification of the 1993 edition when it becomes available, please provide the following information and return it to the appropriate address on the following page.

Name:_____

Company_____

Title_____

Address_____

_____

_____

_____

Telex_____

Telfax_____

Requests for additional copies of this book:

In the United States and countries other than Russia:
TRADEWINDS Press
Address - 1 Closter Commons
Box 400, Suite 140
Closter, New Jersey, 07624, USA
Fax Orders 201-768-4757
Bank ID# ABA 021202162, Acct: Tradewinds Press
Bulk sale discounts available.

In Russia:
The Production-Creative Union <<D.A.H.C.>>
Address - Bldg.3,
Str. Sadovaja-Triumfalnaja 16,
Moscow, USSR
Mailing address -
P.O. Box 30,
2 Tverskaja-Jamskaja 15,
125047, Moscow, USSR
The PCU <<D.A.H.C.>> is in the State Register for
the Foreign Economic Ties Participants under No. -
1145/4186.
Calculations account No. 345013, Transeksopobank
No. 161829 in MGU of GOSBANK of the USSR,
Moscow, MFO 201791.
Currency account with the VNESHECONOMBANK No.
67084308/003 Moscow, MFO 805012
Telex: 411700 <<D.A.H.C.>>
Telefax: (095)292 65 11-<<D.A.H.C.>>
Phone: 209 29 50; 209 29 68; 209 69 76

Publishers Note

At its best, publishing is still a very personal business. Producing a timely and valuable book like **Russia and Its Mysterious Market: Getting Started & Doing Business in the New Russian Marketplace** brings together the energy, creative talent, and good cheer of many special friends. We would like to thank our publishing "partners" in this particular project - Tom, Stan, Denise, Eloise, Pat, Phil, and Brian.

In addition to these individuals, the people at TRADEWINDS Press want to express a special thanks to all of you, our customers. We welcome your comments for improving the quality of our services to you and ideas for future publications.

For Ben, Josh, Katherine, and Samantha and all our children

Each year TRADEWINDS Press donates a portion of our profits to student programs throughout the world which promote cross cultural education and understanding, believing such efforts will lead to improved trade relations in the future.